The Impact of Democracy on Economic Growth:

A Neural Network Approach

Sven Simon

Abstract

A neural network economic output model based on 28 political and economic variables from the Polity IVd and Penn World Table data sets is used to show that democracy has a small but consistently positive influence on economic output. A 1 point increase in "democracy" (on a 0 to 10 scale) results in around a 1% increase in economic output. It is demonstrated that modern neural networks are capable of handling input values outside of the range of data used in their training making them more resilient to unexpected input values.

Dedication

The dedication of this work is not a personal one. This research is dedicated first to the world's impoverished people. The world's poor can benefit the most from methods of analyzing and guiding decisions on the choice of governmental systems. By seeking the knowledge inherent in the empirical data of the experiences of various governments over the last half century, the future of humanity stands to learn the lessons they need to avoid the mistakes of those before them. We, the people of the world, stand to learn nothing less than the facts needed to make the toughest decision of all, the choice of our own governance.

Acknowledgments

I wish to thank the thesis director, Prof. Jeff Gill, for his valuable input, feedback, guidance, patience with my professional responsibilities, and encouragement through the entire process of completing this work. I also wish to thank Harvard University for the privilege and opportunity to learn from and be guided by many outstanding scholars over the last few years. The extraordinary moral characters of the University in providing learning opportunities to dedicated scholars contributes immensely to the well-being of the local and at the same time the most remote, economically impoverished communities of the world.

Table of Contents

List of Figures

List of Tables

Chapter 1 Introduction

Economic growth is a complex subject with many interdependent variables that are difficult to analyze. This complexity is demonstrated practically by the immense disparity in global per capita income and academically by the voluminous cross country studies that encounter contradictory results.

The paper shows that computational techniques involving neural networks can be used to perform analyses of economic growth related data sets. Although there has been a hesitancy and controversy surrounding neural networks in social science research, this has been resolved by mathematical proofs and continued empirical applications.

In this study, neural networks are applied world-wide country financial and regime data commonly used in Political Science. Specifically, a neural network algorithm is applied to a combined data set of macro-economic and financial information from the Penn World Tables[1] and regime characteristic information form Polity IVd[2]. The study demonstrates that neural networks can be helpful in the analysis of economic growth. The model is then applied in a political science context.

In this paper, a neural network economic output model based on 28 political and economic variables from the Polity IVd and Penn World Table data sets is used to show

---

[1] The Penn World Tables are published by the Center for International Comparisons at the University of Pennsylvania, see <http://pwt.econ.upenn.edu/php_site/pwt_index.php> for more information.

[2] Polity IV d is a series of regime characteristic and regime transition data maintained jointly by the University of Maryland and George Mason University, see < http://www.cidcm.umd.edu/inscr/polity/> for more information.

that democracy has a small but consistently positive influence on economic output. It is demonstrated that modern neural networks are capable of handling input values outside of the range of data used in their training making them more resilient to unexpected input values.

Overview

The paper is organized into three general parts: Chapters 2 provides an overview of neural network theory and their recent applications, Chapter 3 provides an overview and review of recent economic growth research, while Chapter 4 presents an application of a commercially available neural network algorithm to the analysis of variables influencing country specific economic output using macroeconomic data from 1950 to 2003. Specifically, the effect of democracy as operationalized in the Polity IVd data tables is analyzed with respect to economic output. Chapter 5 presents a brief summary, avenues for further research, and minor notes.

Chapter 2 Neural Networks: Conclusion of a Controversy

Much hype, excitement, suspicion, disbelief, doubt, and anticipation has surrounded the academic progress of theoretical models based on how scientists believe biological neurons may behave and interact. From a few ideas posited in the 1800s, a class of mathematical and computational models evolved whose role in academia and government is currently solidifying. In order to understand what plausible role, if any, neural networks can have in a research context, the academic history, basic structure, types of networks, mathematical proofs of their behavior, and current applications of these models, are discussed below. The intention is to tie these topics together in an advanced introduction that provides an understanding of the general capabilities and limitations of neural networks.

Introduction

A brief, high-level description of what neural networks[3] are supposed to do is appropriate before delving further into an overview of neural networks. In one sentence, neural networks are supposed to model mathematical functions. Numerically, neural networks are supposed to yield realistic output values for given input values of a known range. The challenge to neural network researchers is to come up ways to create networks that produce output values consistent with "training" data sets. The training data set includes many examples of any number of input values and corresponding single output values. Devising methods of arranging the network is not an easy task as

---

[3] Computational applications of "neural" networks are sometimes called "artificial neural networks" (ANNs).

it should be proven that the network does in fact mimic a function approximating the training set.

Although grounded in ideas related to the biological sciences, today's computational models of how neurons interact to make "decisions" does not require detailed discussion of biochemistry. After an overview of their academic history, neural networks are presented below by progressing in increasing complexity from a single neuron (or "node" to use the less biological term) to more complex networks (and concepts). After presenting the neuron, various types of networks are discussed below. The networks differ primarily in how multiple nodes are configured what the individual neurons do, and how the neurons of the network are configured in a process called "training." A physical description and overview of typically popular networks includes information on how nodes are configured to produce output in the same range as training data, and how the network is trained.   Recent mathematical proofs of the properties of the networks and training algorithms are referenced and briefly discussed. The overview of neural networks is then concluded with a survey of existing applications and the notable absence of their application (or even existence) in political economy literature. Except in the presentation of different types of networks, the discussion is generally intended to focus attention on the most mainstream neural network in use. A technical term used to describe this common network is multi-layered feed forward backpropagation network.

With this introduction, the academic history, types of neural networks, mathematical proofs, and examples of current neural network applications can be presented.

Overview of Neural Network Academic History

In 1943, Warren McCulloch, a neuroscientist, published a paper with Walter Pitts, a "logician," describing the interconnection of a brain cell in mathematical terms. Entitled "A Logical Calculus of the Ideas Immanent in Nervous Activity," it described a binary (on or off) node activated based on a combination of inputs. Research continued by tying this single neuron into networks. Frank Rosenblatt pioneered research on tying similar single nodes (which became known as "perceptrons") into networks. Throughout the late 1950s and early 1960s Rosenblatt explored how they might be arranged and "trained" to yield simple outputs, though training more complex networks turned out to be difficult (Fine 1999:9).

The history of neural networks is shrouded characterized by a rivalry between researchers at Cornell and MIT beginning in the early to mid 1960s. The aftermath of this controversy still lingers in some circles, hampering neural networks acceptance within some academic fields. During the 1960s, two approaches to cognitive science were emerging. On the one hand were McCulloch and Pitts type models exploring how neurologic processes could function to produce intelligence. A competing approach based on symbolic logic was also gaining popularity. Symbolic processing involves breaking sentences and reasoning statements into constituent parts and using formal logic rules to associate them.

The typical historical account of why neural network research dwindled after its initial excitement in the 1940s and 1950s involves a general abandonment of the technique due to inherent theoretical limitations. A roadblock was hit when it was claimed, in 1969, by Minsky and Papert that the standard neural networks of the time, Rosenblatt's perceptrons, were not capable of representing linearly inseparable functions. Minsky and Papert had incorrectly asserted that their conclusions would likely be widely applicable to more complex arrangements of "perceptrons." Unfortunately for neural network research, Minsky and Papert's work was widely accepted. Research funding and interest for the field encountered an inverse relationship to the wide popularity of the publication. Advancement in neural network theory was thereby close to non-existent through the 1970s. Not until the early 1980s did researchers re-embrace neural networks as Minsky and Papert's unfounded extension of the limitations of "single layer" networks to more complex systems was disproven (Maren, Harston, and Pap 1990: 16).

A deeper probe of the dwindling popularity and continued skepticism, in some circles, that neural networks began to encounter during the 1960s reveals much more than the story that neural network research fell out of fashion because it was proven somehow inadequate. In "A Sociological Study of the Official History of the Perceptrons Controversy," Mikel Olazaran details the bitter, almost fanatical academic rivalry that developed between Rosenblatt's "perceptron" camp at Cornell and the symbolic intelligence researchers at MIT. Olzaran explains that Minsky and Papert systematically discredited Rosenblatt by redefining his perceptron very narrowly. The mathematical proofs presented in the Minsky and Papert paper prove that perceptrons are incapable of many things, but they ignore the more complex networks Rosenblatt had devised (Olzeran 1996).

The academic history of the first few decades of rigorous cognitive research after World War II, and even beyond, might be summarized by over enthusiasm leading to disrepute. For a time, Rosenblatt was a media darling hyping the promises of neural networks even to the public. As the *New York Times* reported following a Washington press conference by Rosenblatt, perceptrons were poised to allow computers to "walk, talk, see, write, reproduce itself and be conscious of its existence" (Olazaran 1996: 621).

Such claims were quite lofty and discredited neural networks since these apparently imminent goals were not achieved. Minsky and Papert's symbolic artificial intelligence (AI) approach was not immune to the same disappointment process. The claims were similarly incredible: within ten years (from 1957) thanks to symbolic AI "computers would win the world chess championship, compose aesthetically valuable music, discover and prove an important unknown mathematical theorem, and that most psychological theories would take the form of computer programs" (Olazaran 1996: 623). Ten years passed, promises went unfulfilled, and reasonable people began questioning anything with the term "AI" associated to it. Research continued.

In the 1980s, multiple layers of perceptrons were used to solve the supposed earlier impossibilities of neural networks. Series of nodes were placed between input nodes and output nodes connecting only nodes within the network. These intermediate layer(s) became widely known as "hidden" layers[4] (see Figure below). A successful network training technique, backpropagation, originally proposed by Werbos in 1974 was advanced by Hopfield in 1982 and continually improved over the decade. In previous works, such as a 3 stage network designed by Rosenblatt, the intermediate layer of perceptrons had been referred to as an "association" layer (Maren, Harston, and Pap 1990: 15). In other words, Rosenblatt had considered more complex networks than those that were proven by Minsky and Papert to be of little utility, but he had lacked the techniques to implement them. The resurgent interest and implementation of new

---

[4] An unfortunate term, though widely used, which contributed to the misconception that the technique is analogous to a "black box" where the processes occurring inside of the box are unknown.

training techniques in the 1980s again caused excitement border lining hype (Fine 1999:

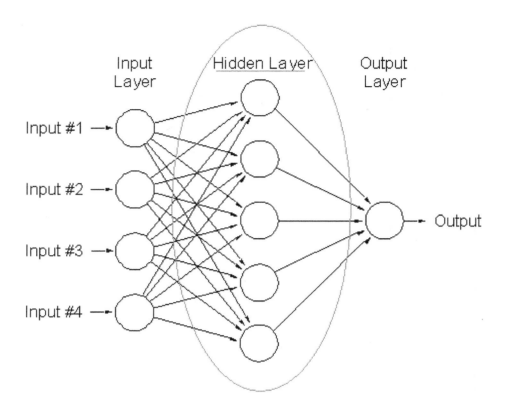

10).

Figure 1: A neural network with a single 'hidden' layer
(<http://smig.usgs.gov/SMIG/features_0902/tualatin_ann.fig3.gif>).

The single most important event in the history of neural networks took place in

1989. That year several now widely cited independent researchers published

mathematical proofs, discussed below, that multilayer neural networks can be used as

universal approximators of mathematical functions (Cybenko 1989; Funahashi 1989;

Hornik, et al. 1989). Overblown promises of neural networks were reigned in and

moderated in the 1990s as much was learned regarding their limitations and capabilities

(Fine 1999: 10).

With this background of the recent academic history of neural networks, a more

detailed look at the neuron, neural network composition and the present frontiers of research can be undertaken. Important concepts of neural networks are presented in this framework.

The Neuron

The "neuron" (or "node" in the Computer Science terminology) is the simplest portion of a neural network. The neuron represents a small computational entity. Typically neurons and the networks they comprise are graphically represented with inputs on the left and outputs on the right. Neurons perform a small series of mathematical operations. A neuron may have one or more inputs (x) each constrained by a weight (w). Neurons with multiple inputs must sum up the products of all input value/weight pairs. A threshold value (θ) is then deducted before this sum of the input values (x_i) is presented to an "activation" function[5] (ϕ) which determines the single current output value of the neuron (y). In the case of a neuron with one input this can be represented as:

$$\phi\,(wx - \theta) = y$$

Graphically:

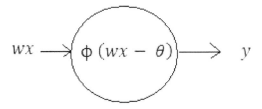

Figure 2: A single network node including operational functions. Input x, weight w, function ϕ, threshold θ, and output y are shown.

---

[5] Like much of neural network terminology there is a diverse nomenclature in circulation for this function. The researcher has also seen examples of this function referred to as a "trigger function," "output function," "transfer function," "characteristic equation", and simply by the class of function used.

In the case of multiple inputs x_1 to x_k which may each have individual weights (w) are summed before the output function is evaluated, we have:

$$\phi \left(\sum_{i=1}^{k} w_i x_i - \theta \right) = y$$

Graphically:

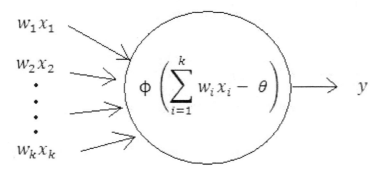

Figure 3: A single node with multiple inputs x_1 to x_k and showing associated weights w, function ϕ, threshold θ, and output y.

The output (y) is the dependent variable. The threshold (θ) is used to constrain the input x to reduce the node's "firing" (i.e. production of an output value) when the input value is low. When $wx - \theta < 0$, y is not realized.

The function (ϕ) computed by the node is the key to understanding what a node does and, as discussed below, what networks based on them are capable of. Popular functions used are in the class of continuous bounded differentiable functions such as trigonometric functions with outputs in ranges of (-1, 1) or (0, 1). Examples of this include sigmoid or logit functions such as

$$f(x) = \frac{1}{1 - e^x}$$

20

and *tanh* (Warner and Misra 1996: 287). These functions are used in the neuron because they ensure continuous (i.e. predictable) output values in the expected range and because the differentiability qualities of these functions have permitted the proofs of their capability of approximating a continuous function derived from the training data set.

Types of Neural Networks

The term neural network can refer to a set of small physical object such as interweaved biological cells, circuits of wires connecting electronic models of "neurons", and, as the term is used in much of this paper, to computer representations of neurons arranged in various configurations. A neural network can be described physically as comprising one or more input nodes arranged to produce one or more outputs. Neural networks differ in three respects: (1) the arrangement (including number) of neurons, (2) the activation function(s) of its neurons, and (3) the methods used to "train" the network.

Network Topology

The arrangement of nodes into a network is the second defining characteristic of a neural network. Many neuron configurations have been devised for various reasons and with varying success.

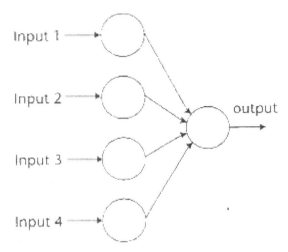

Figure 4: A simple neural network (Tang and MacLennan, 2005: 250).

Figure 4 shows a simple arrangement of neurons. In more complex networks nodes are connected to many intermediate nodes before finally terminating at one or more output nodes[6]. Two simplifications have been widely adopted that makes the networks easier to understand both conceptually and mathematically. First, the intermediate nodes which do not accept input values of the network and that do not represent a final output of the network can be arranged in "layers." This introduces the constraint that nodes in one "layer" are connected only to nodes in layers preceding or following them as shown in Figure 5.

---

[6] More on how many output nodes a network has in a moment.

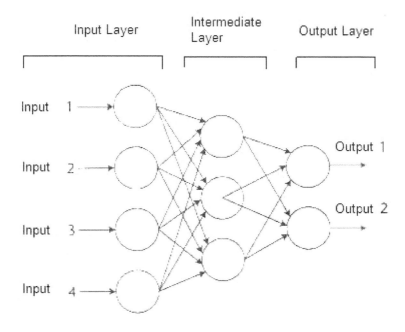

Figure 5: A feed forward network with one "hidden" layer and two outputs (Tang and MacLennan, 2006: 250)

By convention the intermediate layers are frequently referred to as "hidden" layers in the literature. A second common simplification, which can be seen in Figure 5, is that output values propagate only from one layer to the next. That is, output values of any node are never passed back to inputs of nodes in a previous layer. This is what is meant by "feedforward." A "feedback" network, then, is one in which some node outputs do get passed back to nodes which have influenced the values on its own inputs. Since the existence of a feedback connection would make the definition of "layer" of nodes difficult, when neural networks with layers are discussed, feedforward networks can be understood.

Multiple output nodes on the network are possible as seen in Figure 5. However, multiple output nodes are conceptually and computationally analogous to having several single output networks with the same inputs trained on the same data. For simplification purposes it is therefore possible to constrain the number of output neurons to one (Tang and MacLennan 2005: 257). Constraining network outputs to single nodes reduces the mental and mathematical complexity of the network. This reduction to single nodes is graphically depicted in Figure 6 where a multi-output network (a) is broken into two networks, (b) and (c).

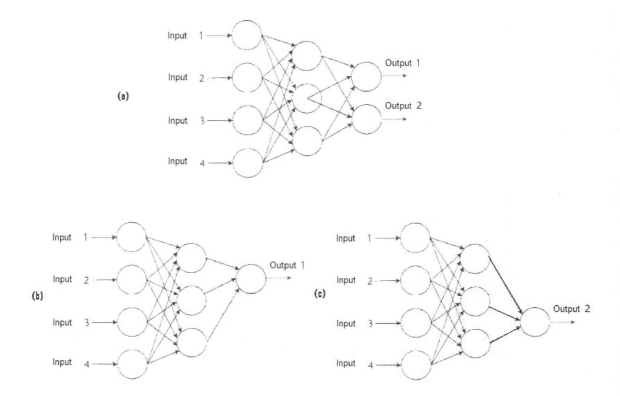

Figure 6: As a simplification, networks with multiple outputs can be reduced to multiple networks with single outputs.

One difficult problem is the question of how many nodes and hidden layers should exist in a neural network. No clear consensus exists on how many layers or hidden layer neurons are optimal. This continues to be an area of ongoing research. Because mathematically a single hidden layer can be expressed in simpler terms and some proofs of neural network utility rely on the constraint of having only one hidden layer, use of a single hidden layer may be preferred where no clear computational advantage is obtained using multiple hidden layers.

Activation Functions

As previously discussed, each node has an activation function. The activation function is typically the same in all neurons of the network, at least across the same layer of neurons. The activation function of the output layer differs from the other neurons in the network. In early research the activation function, a "threshold" function, was used to generate binary outputs (0 or 1). Neural networks based on nodes with threshold functions that have binary outputs are sometimes still referred to by the term "perceptron" that was used by Rosenblatt and others considering such networks. The choice of activation function often is used as the primary identifier of a neural network.

Network Training

Network training is the process by which the weight of each neuron input is adjusted so that a given input combination will result a desired output. Even McCulloch and Pitts in the 1940s considered complex networks, but a process by which weights in multi-layered networks could be reasonably well configured was not devised until Werbos, in 1974, proposed and Hopfield, in 1982, popularized "backpropagation" training.

Although the precise details of how training algorithms propagate error functions backwards from the output and adjust the network's weights accordingly are outside the scope of this chapter, the basics of how computer training algorithms work are important in understanding what trained networks do.

During training, the neural network is unsystematically exposed to a large number of known sample cases of matching input values to output value(s)[7]. Essentially, a single case of input data is fed into the network. The training algorithm

---

[7] A small percentage of the known cases are withheld in order to test the data after training using the majority of data is complete.

25

then compares the output value with the known correct output value and modifies each neuron weight in such a way that the output error is reduced. Training is a computationally expensive operation since each weight must be evaluated for each instance of training data[8]. After a large number of repetitions of this process, if the input data was not random the network becomes capable of approximating outputs based on inputs similar to the training data. The "fitness" of the trained network is tested by using the network to produce output values from the previously withheld real data and comparing it to the real output values.[9]

There are a few problems with neural network training. Some of these problems must be solved by the training algorithm; others must be solved by researchers implementing the network. A large training set is needed in order for the neuron input weights to be generalized. Without an adequate training algorithm, it is possible for networks to simply memorize the input cases. It is also possible for the network to be "overfit" the data. Finally, values radically outside the typical range may be encountered during training.

Mathematical Aspects of Neural Network Fitness

Modern neural networks have been designed to and demonstrated mathematically to avoid radical, discontinuous outputs. The mathematical justification for multi layer feedforward backpropagation networks is provided by the independently derived proofs using several differing approaches of Cybenko; Funahashi; and Hornik, Stinchcombe, and White, (all in 1989). These proofs apply approximation theory to

---

[8] Conversely, however, once the weights are sufficiently determined, using the trained network is very efficient.

[9] This is an example of "supervised" learning.

neural networks to show, in the words of Hornik, et al, that "multilayer feedforward networks are a class of universal approximators."

Today's neural networks are therefore capable of modeling any continuous function and are proven to be capable of doing so as long as the constraints of the proofs are observed[10]. Because these networks utilize trigonometric functions in their activation methods, the range of neural network output values is continuous, bounded and differentiable. These are important properties required of the functions in the proofs.

Understanding the Approximated Function

But what function does a neural network actually approximate? Where does this function come from and how might it be useful?

A satisfying answer to these questions comes from statistics. A neural network with no hidden layers actually computes a logistic regression. The two are mathematically equivalent (Tang and MacLennan 2005, 259). This property carries over to the hidden layer case except that the function modeled by the network can be any continuous function, not linear or log form of a typical regression. As summarized by Warner and Misra (1996) in an article titled "Understanding Neural Networks as Statistical Tools", the answer is generalized that neural networks "can be viewed as a nonparametric regression method" (Warner and Misra 1996: 292). The function modeled by the neural network with hidden layers is a non-linear regression.

As in the case of regression methods it is important to keep in mind that output values of the functions may only be applicable over the same range of values used in its computation (training). The neural network cannot "learn" information which is not provided in the input cases.

---

[10] Note that these proofs apply to the capability of a properly trained neural network but do not vouch for the validity or applicability of training methodologies.

Broad Applications of Neural Networks

Neural networks have now been successfully deployed to solve diverse problems. Although it is out of the scope of this chapter to discuss detailed implementations of neural network applications, a brief survey of the diversity of the problems that neural networks have been utilized for provides a clearer picture of the difficult problems they are capable of solving. Fraser (2006) summarizes some neural network applications:

- o Character recognition
- o Finger print recognition
- o signal recognition (including speech)
- o sonar identification
- o Meteorological classification
- o Automatic vehicle control
- o Diagnosis of hypertension
- o Detection of heart abnormalities
- o Detection of explosives
- o Prediction of bank failure
- o Prediction of stock market performance
- o Prediction of protein secondary structures
- o Credit card theft detection

This is just a small sample of the types of problems neural network solutions have been developed for. In addition, the United States Postal Service uses neural network based character recognition to read zip codes on envelopes and packages.

Neural Networks in Political Economy

Considering neural networks' proven capacity to deal with problems with large, complex data sets it is somewhat surprising that relatively few journal articles can be found specifically using neural networks to study economic statistics and political science. Outside of the traditional natural science fields in which neural networks were first posited (Computer Science, Biology, and Mathematics) neural networks have only recently gained acceptance. Swanson and White, for example, refer to "a novel class of nonlinear models called artificial neural networks" in an article on economic forecasting (Swanson and White 1997: 540). Nevertheless, neural networks do have applications outside the scholarly fields that discuss their theory and mathematics. There are some applications of neural networks in recent scholarly articles. The state failure task force, funded in the mid 1990s by the US Government to study and predict regime failure, uses neural networks to attempt to enhance prediction of impending state failures (King 2001). The Canadian Imperial Bank of Commerce utilizes neural networks to predict Canadian GDP growth and inflation data (Tkacz 2001: 57). Aiken has demonstrated that neural networks can be used to predict the Consumer Price Index using leading economic indicators (Aiken 1999: 296-301).

Although published articles applying neural networks to economic growth theory and even social science in general appear to be relatively few, using neural networks to predict economic variables is not a new idea. Current work applying neural network techniques appears simply to be more popular in the private and government sectors and the natural sciences (including Computer Science and Engineering). The researcher has not found specific mention of using neural network techniques in the identification of necessary variables for economic growth.

There are several problems which contribute to the lack of adoption of neural network methods in the social vs. other sciences. These reasons include confusing nomenclature, less or different mathematical orientation, and the image problems created by the series of broken promises that neural networks and artificial intelligence exemplify.

Terminology problems emanate from the diverse fields and researchers developing neural network theory who develop widely divergent terms. An examples of this is the many terms referring to the activation function. Very field specific terms are used in research papers which originate in different academic fields[11]. The point is that the terminology used in neural network research has not developed the necessary cohesion for it to become easily portable across fields. The second terminology issue is that phrases which have become popular enough to cross academic boundaries are sometimes negative in nature. The term "hidden" layer in reference to the intermediate layer of nodes is not academically appealing to researchers seeking transparency. Labels such as "black box" of a network that proliferated before the internals of neural networks were better explained continue to create barriers.

A second barrier to neural network adoption is the previously mentioned disregard caused by the cycles of unfulfilled hype and promises of the technique early in its life. Warranted or not, Minsky and Papert's campaign against neural networks during the 1960s left a lasting impression that was not remedied by the enthusiasm for neural networks in the 1980s. The recent proofs of neural networks' mathematical fitness cast aside the previous skepticism. Much of this skepticism is now, arguably, unwarranted. Simply because the non-linear equations which the network is capable of representing are difficult to translate into traditional mathematical terms is no longer a reason enough

---

[11] Consider, for example, the layout of a neural network which would be called "network topology" or " network architecture" in Computer Science.

to dismiss their academic value. The capabilities of neural networks for modeling complex mathematical functions can help researcher's understand complex political and economic processes.

Chapter 3 Economic Growth

The application of economic growth theories have not resulted in practical advice that developing governments can heedlessly implement with predictable results. The problem of understanding economic growth processes and devising sound growth strategies continues to be a difficult challenge. These challenges are apparent in economic growth studies which often fall into one of two camps: studies based on theoretical models for which empirical evidence is often in short supply and cross country studies regressing single or multiple variables with often inconclusive results because of selection bias and data consistency problems.

This chapter reviews economic growth from an academic and policy perspective. First, the neoclassical growth model which sparked many academic efforts to understand the mechanics of growth is presented. Then, some of the practical approaches that have been applied to developing countries in an effort to foster economic growth are discussed. Especially the bases of the strategies promoted by international development organizations such as the IMF and World Bank since the 1950s make up this third portion of the chapter. Finally, more recent topics and studies directed to the analysis of economic growth variables are surveyed. Developing countries need robust functional frameworks and tools to understand how they can promote their own well being.

The Neoclassical (Solow) Growth Model

Introduction

Of the many "classical" scholars of development economics such as Roy Forbes Harrod, Joseph Alois Schumpeter, Ragnar Nurkse, Theodore Schultz, and Robert Solow, particularly Robert Solow's work has inspired a plethora of further growth scholarship. His growth model, synonymously called the neoclassical, Solow, and sometimes the Solow-Swan model, is credited with sparking a wave of research spanning many decades. The model is typically taught at the university level in both economic growth and even introductory macroeconomics courses (Taylor 2000). For his contributions to development economics, Robert Solow was awarded the Nobel Prize in 1987.

The neoclassical growth model that Solow devised in the late 1950s is based on a production function with labor and capital as its primary inputs. It also contains a third residual value that accounts for the difference between an economy's actual economic growth and the growth expected from labor and capital. A process called growth accounting tracks how much output growth is expected from different inputs. Growth accounting is the mathematical attempt to operationalize economic growth into various constituent parts. Extensions to Solow's theoretical model attempt to devise (often very sophisticated) mathematical ways to account for additional growth related variables.

In this section the basics of the neoclassical growth model and some of its more recent theoretical extensions are presented. This provides the background for a brief survey of economic growth studies by topic.

Basics of the Model

The basics of the neoclassical growth model revolve around a production function containing labor (L), capital (K), and a third variable (A) which has been given various names. The Solow model is based on a production function like Equation 3.1, typically referred to as a Cobb-Douglas production function[12].

$$Y = AK^{\alpha}L^{1-\alpha}$$

Eq. (3.1)

The assumptions which are embedded in the Solow model are important to enumerate. These assumptions were based on observations of the US and major developed economies. The set of these observations were attributed to British economist Nicholas Kaldor. The observations include that (1) the percentage level of labor and capital in the economy, (2) the capital output ratio, and (3) return on capital are near constant in the long run. Further, (4) output per worker (Y/L) and capital per worker (K/L) grow at a constant, positive rate. These presumptions of the Solow growth model are believed to hold for industrial countries over the last century (Doepke: 2003).

The major characteristics of the model, in addition to incorporating the above presumptions, include decreasing returns to labor and capital, depreciation of capital, and the existence of a steady state in which capital depreciation and the labor growth rate[13] offset each other. These characteristics can be seen graphically in Figure 3.1 which graphs output per worker, y, vs. capital per worker, k.

---

[12] Where α ranges from 0 to 1.
[13] Population growth and "laborer growth" rate are used interchangeably. In other words, the population growth rate is used as a measure of the increase or decrease in the labor force.

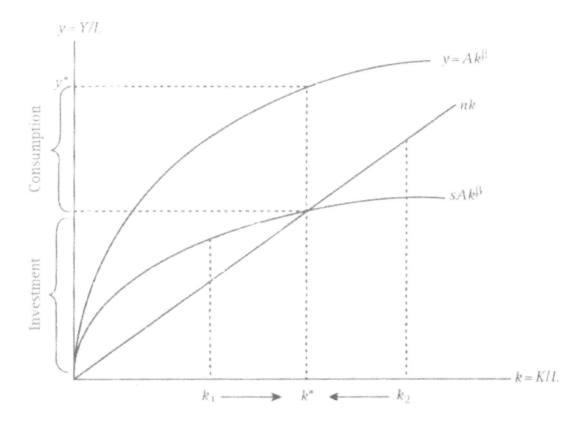

Figure 3.1: The Solow growth model. (Source: Hayami and Godo, p. 143)

In devising the model, Solow was attempting to explain the relationship between capital accumulation and growth (Helpman, 2005: 12). He did this by deriving an equation for the change in capital from equation 3.1. Specifically, Solow showed that the change in capital equals investment minus depreciation (equation 3.2)[14] (Jones, 1998: 22).

$$\dot{K} = sY - dK \qquad \qquad \text{Eq. (3.2)}$$

What the model shows contradicts the "capital fundamentalist" view that growth can be achieved through investment. Because labor and capital must grow at proportionate rates, a short term boost in capital (a move from k* to k_2 in Figure 3.1, for example) will

[14] Note that in growth economics derivatives are sometimes written in a dot notation. In equation 3.2, for example writing *dK/dt* instead of $\dot{K}$ would have given *dK* a different meaning than the intended "depreciation rate multiplied by capital stock."

not have a large effect on output per worker (y). Therefore, not much growth will occur simply because more capital is available to workers. Instead, the return per unit of capital will be lowered.

The Solow growth model is standard materials in economics books and university classrooms. Much of this longevity has to do with the versatility of its composition. The third variable, referenced as A in the model's production function (equation 3.1) was described by Solow as "technology", but is also often referred to as "Total Factor Productivity" (TFP or "productivity") and sometimes simply as the "Solow residual." These varying definitions speak for its ambiguity. 'A' has an overarching impact on the results of the economic output reported by the production function. The role of technology/productivity in growth became a much discussed topic in the decades following the presentation of the Solow model. Explanations of different types of technologies and productivity that can help economic output have been extended in many directions over the years. Technology can mean not only new machinery, but also inventions and business processes that arrange capital and labor in more productive ways.

The need to explain A, which Solow (1957) noted as containing the majority of economic growth, led to a process called growth accounting in which the year over year change in economic output is broken down between labor, capital, and other factors.

Augmented/Endogenous Solow Models

Some of the extensions (often called "augmentations") to the Solow model focus on "endogenous" variables from within the economy. Most of these extensions have not made a lasting theoretical impact on growth theory because they have not been consistently able to explain growth patterns in empirical studies[15]. A small number of

---

[15] See, for example, Pack (1994).

scholars do stand out for reinvigorating the growth scholarship in the late 1980s and early 1990s. The two most prominent were Lucas and Romer who both focused on variables endogenous to an economy. Lucas focused on the effect of human capital accumulation beginning with Lucas (1988). Romer (1990) constructed elaborate models of the impact of R&D based on the Solow model even including temporary monopoly powers granted to firms through patent and trade secret institutions. Mankiw, Romer, and Weil (1992) even managed to create an augmented Solow model integrating human capital *does* appear consistent with cross country empirical data. The Solow model may have been used as the basis or justification for some policy decisions. For example, the model provides justification for checks on population growth since an increase in the population (i.e. worker) growth rate without an accompanying increase in capital growth would decrease the labor/capital ratio resulting in drops of productivity.

Growth Strategies in Practice

Economists' and policy maker's approach to increasing economic growth over the last century can be characterized as a search for a holy grail that might unleash growth. Various strategies were identified, popularized, and implemented on grand scales by the World Bank and International Monetary Fund. In the 1960s, for example, education was believed (or hoped) to be the key to growth. Other "keys" to growth that were almost experimentally invested in on grand scales range from the general infusion of tremendous quantities of foreign aid, capital accumulation, the control of population growth, and in the last few decades debt forgiveness. Each time one growth policy was found not be the ultimate growth catalyst, other requisite variables were added or substituted to the current vogue. By the early 1990s, the list of policies thought by World

Bank and IMF policy makers to be necessary to set underdeveloped states on the right path grew to around ten. This list became popularly known as the "Washington Consensus". However, even this combined list of seemingly prudent policies failed to bring growth to much of the world.

In his book *The Elusive Quest for Growth*, former World Bank economist William Easterly summarizes some of the serious approaches that international institutions funded by OECD nations have taken in promoting growth in the developing world since the 1950s. Initially, a Keynesian approach to stimulating growth was taken. Funds were made available for investment in machinery. Subsequently, education, population control, privatization, specific policy reforms, and finally debt forgiveness were each treated as potential "elixirs" for growth (Easterly 2001: 23).

Recent Topics in Economic Growth

A plethora of research searching for variables that impact economic growth can be found in current scholarly circles. This research is often framed around popular development theories in particular, still, the Solow growth model.

In this section a survey of a portion of the recent scholarship surrounding which variables influence economic growth is presented. Because of the overwhelming number of variables that have been studied with respect to economic growth in recent years, even such a survey must be selective about which variables to address. Durlauf, Johnson and Temple have noted that the number of growth regressors that have been used to explain growth in recent studies nearly rival the number of countries in the world (Durlauf *et al.* 2004: 75). Conceptually it is helpful to think of recent studies in three broad categories: cross country growth regressions, studies using Solow based determinants, and studies with non-Solow based growth determinants. This is a mental separation used by Durlauf, Johnson and Temple in grouping the results of recent growth studies in appendixes to a recent working paper (Durlauf *et al.* 2004: 139-156). The reader is referred to these appendixes for a generous[16] list of recently studied variables. A thorough coverage of even a sizable majority of these variables is outside the scope of this paper. The discussion is constrained to areas which have received disproportionately large amount of recent attention, in which recent breakthrough have been made or claimed, and variables with the most robust cross country data sets.

While past research focused on already mentioned factors such as capital accumulation, education, "technology", and population growth some of the more current topics in economic growth involve the effects of democracy, political institutions, socio-political stability, and trade. Empirical results from growth studies in recent years has led to the general conclusion that to explain economic performance political and social factors such as political institutions and social factors must be considered (Barro and McCleary 2003: 1). The following discussion begins with democracy and presents growth evidence regarding political institutions and socio-economic stability, fundamental areas which have been focal points of recent research.

Democracy and Growth

The effect of the presence of "democracy" alone has not been shown to result in consistent and significant positive growth across studies. Positive externalities of democracy such as the existence of reliable political institutions and constitutional management of social conflict do, however, have an important stabilizing effect on economies, it is claimed. A thorough analysis by Feng (2003) concluded that although positive, the relationship between democracy and growth is statistically insignificant. Instead, the book asserts that the positive contributions of democracy manifest

---

[16] The cross country regression variables list includes studies using over 130 variables.

39

themselves through democracy's "impacts on political instability, policy uncertainty, investment, education, property rights, and birth rates" (Feng 2003: 296). Quinn and Woolley (2001) performed a comprehensive survey of democracy and growth research. They mention contributions by various researchers totaling 45 studies. The result of these studies was that 8 found a negative democracy/growth relationship, 14 a positive relationship, and the remaining 23 somewhere between positive and negative.

In a recent article in the journal *Foreign Affairs*, democracy in India is even presented as exhibiting a barrier to growth. The argument is that the small minority English speaking elite are constrained from making major economic changes by the electoral mass. Small quiet changes continue to be made, but major reforms such as changing labor laws, privatization, reducing farm subsidies and others that might be unpopular in the short and yet make significant positive long term impacts have not gained acceptance. However, it is affirmed and appreciated by the author of the article that the long term stability and rule of law enshrined in India's democratic institutions generate long term growth (Varshney 2007: 93-106).

Political Institutions

Political institutions are the mechanisms that define societal rules, procedures and their enforcement. Recent research on economic growth was directed towards the consideration of the effect of basic institutions on growth by several works by Douglas North in the early 1990s. Institutions are devised to "create order and reduce uncertainty in exchange" (North 1991: 97). Though political institutions are also informal, their formal variants include the rule of law, property rights, and constitutions. Though the idea that individually these political institutions would be beneficial to growth is not new, what is new is the conclusion by several recent studies that institutions have a far greater positive impact on growth than both economic integration and geography (Rodrik *et al.* 2004; Acemoglu *et al.* 2005). The role of geography, however, has not been dismissed as not playing a role. Many studies are quite capable of generalizing growth patterns on a regional basis. Sub-saharan Africa, for example, has seen sub-par growth while many East Asian countries perform better than average. What is claimed is that institutions offer a better explanation for growth than geography in most cases. Further, Rodrik asserts that there is now wide agreement among economic growth scholars that "institutional quality holds the key to prevailing patterns of economic growth around the world"[17] (Rodrik 2004: 1). More specifically in the area of institutions, civil and property rights, high degrees of economic and political freedom, and low levels of corruption have been linked to greater prosperity (Bénassy-Quéré *et al.* 2005).

Building political institutions for growth can be considered as much a problem of nation building as of economic growth. Evans and Rauch (1999) examined the role bureaucratic authority structures play in growth. Reviewing 35 developing countries over 20 years, they found that data measuring the scale at which bureaucracies in the respective countries "employ meritocratic recruitment and offer predictable, long-term careers" significantly enhanced the countries subsequent growth outlook (Evans and Rauch 1999: 748).

Arguably, the reason for institutional importance is that the existence of some degree of national cohesion and security is a prerequisite for growth and for the preservation of accumulated wealth.

Political Instability, Social Disturbance and Growth

Economic output can be reduced by political instability often caused by social

---

[17] Emphasis added.

41

conflict. However, even violently attained regime change can sometimes be good for growth. Easterly and Levine (1997) utilized the number of assassinations in various states to proxy social disturbance as a factor influencing economic growth and suggest that political assassinations are negatively correlated with long run growth in Africa (Easterly and Levine 1997: 1209). Alesina and Perotti (1993) combined the number of assassinations, deaths, coups, and demonstrations to index political instability. Alesina went on to study regime change in relation to instability and found that in times of "high propensity of government collapse, growth is significantly lower than otherwise (Alesina *et al.* 1996). Another study by Collier and Gunning (1999) used the number of months of war to operationalize social disturbance. Fosu (2001) focused on coup plots sub-dived by successful, abortive, and officially reported coup attempts. Social disturbance and the political instability it causes have a negative impact on economic growth in many findings. Fosu's coup finding, on the other hand, found a positive correlation between coups and subsequent economic progress. Indeed, it can be economic trouble that leads to conflict in the first place. One study quantifying this relationship found that a negative growth shock of five percent increased the likelihood of conflict by fifty percent the following year (Miguel *et al.* 2004). Regime change alone is not necessarily "bad." However, prolonged social conflict has long term negative impacts.

One final variable related to stability, though not necessarily social disturbance is exchange rate volatility. In a floating exchange rate system, a state's exchange rate volatility might be considered a proxy for its political and economic stability. Esquivel and Larrain (2002:18) relate exchange rate volatility to economic growth and find that exchange rate volatility (as an independent variable) has a negative impact on exports. In particular, they state that a 1 percent change in G-3[18] exchange rate volatility leads to

---

[18] G-3 is a free trade agreement between Mexico, Colombia and Venezuela.

a corresponding 2 percent decrease in real exports. Further, G-3 exchange rate volatility increases the likelihood of currency crises in the states. This brings us to trade.

Trade, Economic Integration, and the Democratic Peace

One way of reducing conflict between states has long thought to be the economic interdependence promoted by inter-state trade. At its apex trade interdependence is aimed at complete market integration. Such interdependence was promoted in Europe after World War II and led to the establishment and enlargement of the European Union. A widely discussed phenomenon for which empirical evidence appeared in the second half of the twentieth century is the democratic peace, the idea that democratic countries[19] do not have wars with each other. Mousseau (2000) has re-cast democratic peace theory in terms of economic development showing potential weaknesses in the democratic peace ideal. He shows that "the pacifying impact of democracy" holds robustly only as the level of development increases. At low levels of development, the pacifying effect becomes statistically insignificant (Mousseau 2000: 496-497). Even more alarmingly, in a study of trade ties extreme interdependence has been found to increase the likelihood of interstate militarized conflict (Barbieri 1996).

Data Problems Hindering Progress in Growth Theory

Researchers and analysts interpreting economic growth research face substantial challenges in data availability, quality, comparability, and significance. Statistics from especially small undeveloped countries are in short supply. When figures are available they may only be available for small discontinuous time samples. Even the available statistics from one country are often created using widely divergent techniques.

---

[19] A precise definition of democracy is put aside in the present analysis though the reader is encouraged to consult the vast literature on democracy and democratic peace theory.

Data analysis cannot be conducted when data for the same variable is not comparable. Robust, statistically significant, conclusions cannot be drawn from small data sets. Studies conducted on small data sets are easy to discount because of their inherent selection bias. Researchers seeking to study the impact of growth variables are faced with serious data availability, quality, comparability, and significance problems.

Conclusion

Different studies of the same growth related variable often discover positive relationships, no significant relationships, and negative relationships for the same variable. The examples offered here including the sometimes positive impacts of democracy on growth, the sometimes positive impacts of stability, and the usually positive impact of economic integration, is only a very small subset of the plethora of studies in economic growth which daily produce seemingly contradictory empirical results.

One point to take away from this brief survey of recent economic growth related studies is that different findings of the impact for a variable are not proof that the studies conducting the analyses are contradictory. Rather, the studies in question may simply be seeing different effects that the variable can have in different circumstances and using even slightly different methodology. Such varying results are difficult to interpret. Limited data sets involving very small amounts of samples have predisposed many growth studies to selection bias which contributes to the divergence and lack of concrete conclusions.

Conclusion

Scholars of economic growth have only recently been able to agree on some very basic variables such as the existence of political institutions as being beneficial to growth. Theoretical advances in economic growth have been slow. New ideas are slow to take hold because they are difficult to substantiate empirically in a small universe of countries. At the same time, new theories are easily "disproven" by merely applying them to any small subset of data points for which they do not hold. This theoretical environment has given basically only the Solow growth model with its all inclusive, almost hand-waving, "technology"/"productivity" term any academic longevity.

Few if any economic growth models that can be applied in a policy environment have been devised. The lack of academic and practical progress in understanding growth variables has led international organizations to alter their approach towards development assistance. The previous "one size fits all" policy in the international organizations has evolved towards a more individualized, country based approach.

Considering the distressful conditions in which billions of the world's people live, the contradictory and slow progress of the important field of economic growth is distressing. The vast resources working on the problem of economic growth should try to better organize to reduce wasted effort. The use of industry standard computational tools in combination with peer generated statistics might be one step to make studies more easily reproducible. The spectrum of tasks necessary to tackle such a difficult problem is almost too overwhelming for most individual researchers.

In the next chapter, a model of economic output designed to mitigate some of the data problems are used to analyze the effect of democracy on growth. An industry standard software package is used to perform calculations using dozens of variables in thousands of cases. The recent advances in computational "horse power" that allows large quantities of statistics to be analyzed simultaneously can be used to try to understand and utilize data sets and data relationships in new, reliable ways.

Chapter 4 Neural Networks, Democracy, and Economic Output

In this chapter a neural network model is constructed using a data set of over 3000 potential input cases from the Penn World Tables (PWT) 6.2 and Polity IVd data tables. The model is then applied to a recently popular question in political theory. The recent conclusion that democracy may have a weak but positive effect on economic growth is substantiated by testing the effects of a change in the levels of democracy on economic output using a neural network model.

The first portion of the chapter includes detailed information on the neural network model. Fitness of the neural network is evaluated, r^2 of the model output for 2003 data is 0.73, p is 0.85. The subsequent section describes an experiment in which the democracy input values are altered to evaluate the change in economic outputs predicted by the neural network model model at different levels of democracy for 68 countries in 2003. The model demonstrates a consistent positive effect to a change in democracy, supporting the conclusion of many related studies noted in Feng (2003) that democracy has a beneficial impact on economic output[20]. The final portion of the chapter offers some analysis of and insights drawn from the numeric experiments. The qualitative portion of the analysis is then carried forward into chapter 5.

---

[20] Only 2 of the 68 countries exhibited other results: Iraq and the Guinea-Bissau.

The Neural Network Economic Output Model Basics

The model used in the analysis in this chapter consists of a neural network created using a commercial software package, SQL Server 2005. This section reviews some basic ideas behind the model including basic function, choice of the unit of analysis, input variables and data sets, the software used for model creation, the methods used to evaluate model fitness, and miscellaneous potential problems that were taken into account in its design.

The goal is a model that can take various political and economic inputs of a single country in one time period and from those inputs construct an estimate of the economic output expected for that country at that time. Such a model could, for example, be used to identify countries that are under or over-performing economically based on the difference between the expected economic output reported by the model and the actual output observed in the country. Such a model can also be used to do analyses of changes in the input political and economic variables. The model can be used to quantify the effects of a change in an input variable, such as democracy.

Increasing the Size of the Training Data Set

One basic idea behind the neural network model in this paper is that by abstracting away the time series variable ("year") from the analysis, the data set can be increased. A larger data set helps to reduce selection bias. Removing time series also mitigates the danger that the neural network model memorizes input cases instead of generalizing an output function. The strategy of removing the time dimension does present some compromise as historical data might be overemphasized in the outputs of models. However, the initial premise of the idea of this computational model is that the effects of as many political and economic variables as possible in as many possible cases be included in the model. This selection bias avoidance strategy should allow conclusions based on the model(s) to have a broad range.

The basic function of the model(s) is to take many economic and political input variables to produce an estimate of economic output. Specifically, the output variable estimated by the models is real GDP per capita (CGDP) vs. a US benchmark of 100.

Unit of Analysis

The decision on what unit of analysis to use when studying economic growth often depends on what data is available. Intra-country data is often only available in larger countries. Since economic data tends to be available on a country by country basis, collections of country statistics for individual years are the focus of analysis.

Data Set and Input Variables

In the past, limitations of data sets and computational abilities have forced analysts to constrict the number of input cases used in their studies. Recent compilations of political and economic data, however, have managed to cover many countries over many decades. At the same time, the recent advances in computational "horse power" have allowed large quantities of statistics to be analyzed. The data used in this study comes from *The Penn World Table* (versions 6.2) published by the Center for International Comparisons at the University of Pennsylvania and the Polity IVd data set from the Center for International Development and Conflict Management, University of Maryland. *The Penn World Table* provides a set of around thirty macro economic variables for over 160 countries for the period 1950-2003. Polity IVd contains data on political regimes "institutionalized authority characteristics"[21] including variables such as

---

[21] See <http://www.cidcm.umd.edu/polity/about/>

democracy, autocracy, and regime transitions. Both these tables have been used in widely published economic growth related studies.

Input variables for the neural network model are drawn from these two data sets by choosing all data rows from the data sets that have equivalent data for a specific country in a specific year available in both tables. In other words, if data for a country in a specific year is present in both tables, it is used. Some modifications of the Polity IVd were done to accomplish this. Some "country code" values which did not match the country codes in the *Penn World Table* were modified.[22] Beyond these corrections no numeric data was changed with one exception. Many Polity IVd values were coded with non-continuous negative values in cases where regime change or other factors preclude an estimation of the individual values. In these cases the Polity IVd table contained the numbers -88, -77, and -66. These values were removed from all data columns except the regime change columns in which they originate. A 'NULL' value was inserted in their place.

Both data tables were inserted into a SQL Server 2005 database and made available in combined format using a database view resulting in a total of 3172 country/year data rows. As mentioned, the criterion for inclusion of a country/year in the combined data view was the existence of the same country/year row in both data tables.

The variables from the combined Polity/Penn World data table that were used to construct the model are (in alphabetical order): Consumption Share of CGPD[sic], Consumption Share of RGDPL, Democracy, Executive Constraints Concept, Executive Constraints, Executive Recruitment Concept, Government Share Of CGDP, Government Share of RGDPL, Investment Share of CGDP, Investment Share of RGDPL, Openness, Openness in Current Prices, Participation Competitiveness, Participation Regulation,

---

[22] SQL code for performing these operations is available from the author.

Political Competition Concept, Polity Score 2, Population, Price Level of Consumption, Price Level of GDP, Price Level of Government, Price Level of Investment, Prior Polity Code, Ratio of GNP to GDP, Regime Durability, Regime Transition, Regime Transition Completed, State Failure, and Total Change in Polity Value. That comes to a total of 28 variables used as model inputs.

A few explanatory notes regarding the variables. The "Polity Score 2" values are equivalent to "Polity Score" except that the "Polity Score 2" value is normalized to remove non-continuous codes that are used for state failure and regime transition. All variables are treated as continuous. The combination Polity/Penn World Table data set has more variables than the ones chosen. The input variables for the models in figure 7 were selected to exclude any that might contain GDP in their calculations and through a laborious process of building neural networks and seeing which variables increased the accuracy of the network output.

Model Output: Economic Output vs. Economic Growth

Although many studies have attempted to find explanatory variables for what causes "economic growth," values analyzed in this study focus on annual per capita economic output (CGDP) and not a percentage change of output vs. a prior year that might more accurately be called economic "growth". There are a couple of reasons for focusing on output instead of growth. First, economic growth is something that can really only be analyzed in a time series fashion. Output in one period is compared to output in a second period and the percentage difference over several periods can be determined. Because time, the variable "year", has been abstracted away from the model, a percentage change vs. a previous year doesn't exist anymore. This is not really a problem, however. Abstracting to economic output instead of growth may even simplify analysis. In fact, the latest version of the Penn World Table includes a growth variable ("Growth Rate of Real GDP") which, when included in the neural network training actually reduced the accuracy of predicted output. Insofar as economic growth can be understood as the derivative of economic output, growth is a more complex variable than economic output. Abstracting to the lower level of economic output is therefore a welcome simplification. Since the two numbers are intrinsically linked, this paper sometimes refers to output and growth synonymously. Finally, the goal of a developing economy does not need to be how it can become the fastest growing economy ever devised, it merely needs to grow. Economic output is a sufficient and simpler measure of analysis than economic growth.

Use of Commercial Data Analysis Tools

Microsoft SQL Server 2005 and its Analysis Services components were used to construct the models and to adjust the democracy data for the study. This software is available free of charge to students (including the author) in many computer science academic programs. Other software such as SPSS or the new Mathematica 6 could also have been used. Beyond the obvious free availability factor to the author, the benefit of using a commercial tool, and in this case a commercially available neural network algorithm, is twofold. First, the use of existing algorithms reduces the probability of mistakes in mishandling data that might occur in a custom neural network algorithm implementation that has not been tested on a large scale[23]. Second, Microsoft SQL Server 2005 offered the author the opportunity to work with a somewhat familiar interface reducing some of the time otherwise spent trying to work with the software instead of focusing on the research.

---

[23] Insufficiently tested software for the purposes of this research might also include some open source neural network implementations, though not SPSS or Mathematica.

Model Fitness

Two primary values are used to determine model fitness in this study. One is a "score" automatically assigned to each model, and the other is the r^2 value computed using predicted economic output data vs. actual economic output as reported by the Penn World Table in a sample year.

The r^2 value is the square of the Pearson product moment correlation coefficient computed using by squaring the following formula:

$$r = \frac{\sum (x - \bar{x})(y - \bar{y})}{\sqrt{\sum (x - \bar{x})^2 \sum (y - \bar{y})^2}}$$

Figure 7: Pearson product moment correlation coefficient.

x and y, above, represent the average of all x and y values, respectively. Other model fitness related statistics are provided below.

Potential Model Problems

There were several potential problems with the data analysis in this paper that were consciously taken into account in its design. Some of these potential problems have been pointed out, but deserve brief acknowledgement in context with the others mentioned here. The potential problems that were identified and for which specific mitigation strategies were implemented include data set "breadth" to avoid selection bias (for which a reasonably large data set was constructed), models memorizing data (for which certain input variables were excluded), data accuracy (for which the source data sets were selected), and falsifiability (for which commercial algorithms are used and changes to the data sets are documented).

The Model

This section presents the details of the neural network economic output model. Details of the algorithm parameters,

Creating the Model

The neural network model is trained with Polity IVd and Penn World Table (PWT) 6.2 input values from 1950 to 2003 without including time series information. The resulting model is exposed to input data from a recent year (2003) to generate CGDP estimates for 68 countries[24]. These estimates are compared to actual CGDP values from the same year to evaluate model fitness. The below figure graphing actual CGDP values vs. figures from the model outputs show the model's "prediction" of economic output vs. actual economic output in 2003.

---

[24] All countries with CGDP values available in the Penn World Table for 2003 excluding the US and two natural resource rich countries, Saudi Arabia and Qatar, for which the model constantly underestimates economic output.

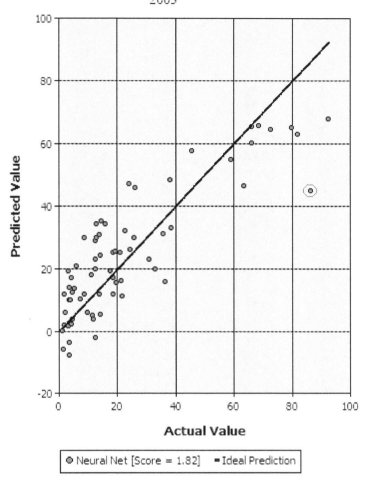

Scatter Plot of Neural Network Predicted vs. Actual CGDP 2003

Figure 8: Neural Network baseline: scatter plot of "predicted" economic output vs. actual economic output (CGDP in % vs US 100) for 68 countries (r^2 = 0.73, p = 0.85).

r^2 of the neural network model's estimated ("predicted") CGDP vs. actual CGDP for the values in Figure 7 (data listed in the table below) is 0.73, p is 0.85.

Table 1: Neural Network predicted vs. actual CGDP relative to US (2003).

	CGDP Relative To US	
Country	Predicted	Actual
Canada	65.15	79.80
Cuba	11.88	18.43
Dominican Rep	15.71	19.43
Jamaica	29.25	12.33
Mexico	32.23	22.74
Nicaragua	6.16	9.57

Panama	47.23	24.10
Colombia	19.48	17.31
Venezuela	25.43	18.49
Ecuador	20.15	12.33
Peru	23.25	12.44
Brazil	25.26	20.91
Bolivia	12.09	8.69
Chile	31.32	35.54
Argentina	23.31	30.66
Belgium	64.56	72.47
Switzerland	30.08	25.68
Poland	45.86	26.17
Austria	62.87	81.98
Hungary	48.50	38.18
Italy	60.10	66.15
Albania	30.03	12.50
Macedonia	44.83	86.19
Slovenia	30.88	13.53
Greece	57.77	45.47
Cyprus	46.48	63.50
Russia	20.25	32.74
Estonia	33.19	38.21
Ukraine	17.18	18.46
Belarus	16.04	36.46
Armenia	5.40	14.05
Azerbaijan	18.23	11.09
Finland	65.63	66.05
Norway	67.91	92.54
Guinea-Bissau	2.21	1.71
Mali	10.13	3.32
Senegal	13.83	5.22
Benin	10.12	3.68
Liberia	0.06	0.98
Ghana	12.56	4.59
Gabon	26.20	24.41
Uganda	1.69	3.17
Kenya	14.22	3.47
Rwanda	-3.41	3.42
Somalia	6.26	1.96
Djibouti	-2.11	12.43
Eritrea	-5.85	1.51
Comoros	3.86	4.37
Tunisia	11.29	21.66
Iran	25.80	19.31
Turkey	34.27	15.82
Iraq	-7.65	3.52
Egypt	12.00	13.67
Syria	21.10	5.90
Jordan	3.92	11.60
Israel	55.03	58.91

Yemen	19.58	3.18
Afghanistan	11.91	1.68
Turkmenistan	16.39	21.23
Uzbekistan	5.24	11.28
China	35.48	14.26
Korea North	2.42	4.09
Japan	65.90	68.41
India	29.98	8.61
Pakistan	10.42	7.18
Laos	17.17	4.05
Papua New Guinea	34.39	12.60
Fiji	24.59	14.13

Most predicted values make sense considering the input data available to the neural network. Large developing countries like India and China with large populations fared worse than the potential the model identifies in them, managing 8.61 % and 14.26 % of US GDP vs. their predicted output of around 30 % and 35 % of US GDP in 2003. Small island countries like Fiji, and Papa New Guinea also managed less economic output than the model predicts based on the political and economic data available[25]. Some countries, like Macedonia, managed almost twice as much output than the short term of its government might lead the neural network to predict. The unusually high Macedonia number (circled in the right side of Figure 7) can be attributed to the stability that EU troops and massive reconstruction aid have brought to the Balkans.

Note that "prediction" in this sense is a bit of a misnomer. Post-diction would be a more accurate term. Further, if actual post-diction were the goal using this model, input data from the time period being post-dicted would not be included in the training data. This model, however, will be used to analyze the effect of changes on inputs. Therefore, the interest lies in having the model internalize as much data as possible without memorizing it. The plot in figure 7 demonstrates that the neural network trained

---

[25] Perhaps the inclusion of some geographic factors in the data could allow the neural network to be more sensitive to an "island" factor.

with all available data is quite capable of estimating economic output at the very least within the time period of its training data.

Algorithm Parameters

Before moving, a brief mention of the default parameters used to create the model. The Microsoft Neural Network can be tweaked in several respects, including the number of hidden nodes in its hidden layer, the maximum number of allowed input variables, the percentage of input cases used to test the model internally, and other settings. The number of hidden nodes in the single hidden layer of the neural network in this case was 22. The default value for the number of hidden nodes is four times the square root of the number of input variables, in the case of single output networks. Some attempts were made to tweak default algorithm parameters to improve network accuracy. However, differences in the accuracy of network output were much more pronounced when changing the input variable selection. Therefore, the default values for the neural network algorithm parameters were used. For further technical details on other default parameters of the Microsoft Neural Network see Tang and MacLennan (2005).

Conclusion

The essentials of the model used in this study is that it is a neural network created from a combined sample of Polity IVd and Penn World Table political and economic data from 1950 – 2003 using Microsoft SQL Server 2005 Analysis Services. It is designed to accept 28 input variables to estimate any country's economic output.

Democracy and Economic Output

The neural network model is now used to evaluate the economic output of 68 countries at various levels of democracy. The model described in the previous section, created using data from 1950 to 2003, is exposed to data in the input data series for 2003 except that the 'democracy' variables (actual values can range from 0, low, to 10, high) are systematically changed. In almost every instance country in the sample, an increase in democracy results in a prediction of greater economic output while a decrease in the democracy level leads to an analogous decrease in economic output.

Approach

The general approach of this experiment has two simultaneous goals. First, is the confirmation and exploration of recent political science claims that democracy does have a positive impact on economic growth despite the presence of conflicting studies. Second, is the demonstration of state of the art neural networks' capacity to continue to provide outputs in a continuous fashion when they are exposed to input data in ranges not experienced in their training. The uncertainty of discontinuous output variables was a major factor in the slow acceptance of neural networks as academic tools earlier in their academic history.

The experiment for this section involved running the neural network economic output prediction for 68 countries in 2003 with different values of democracy for each country. More specifically, for each country in the sample the economic output predicted by the neural model was recorded for 7 potential cases. First, the predicted economic output based on the Polity IVd and Penn World Table data was recorded. Then, the model's output at democracy levels at two integer increments was measured up to democracy value changes +/- 6 above and below the actual democracy value of the particular country being evaluated.

Before delving further into the experiment, a discussion of what is meant by "democracy", and especially how it is defined in the data set is necessary. The definition of the democracy value given in the Polity IVd data set is first the "presence of institutions and procedures" that allow citizens to voice their opinions regarding the efficacy of potential or existing leaders and policies, second is the "existence of institutionalized constraints" that limit the omnipotence of the executive branch[26], and finally the extent to which civil liberties of citizens are protected (Marshall and Jaggers, 2002: 13). This definition has some implications worth mentioning immediately. The other democracy studies that may have had results in which democracy did not have a positive influence on economic growth may have had widely differing definitions of democracy. Those definitions and the data used in the studies would have to be reviewed carefully both to disprove them, but also to include them as evidence contradicting any conclusions offered in this paper regarding democracy's impact on economic output. It is not the goal of this paper to disprove those studies, rather the assertion will be made that the definition and criteria used for democracy in the Polity IVd data set are widely accepted. The conclusions presented should therefore have a more widely applicable impact than those studies founded upon more cursory, definitions. The researcher will hereby humbly disassociate himself with the compilation of the democracy data used and democracy's definition[27]. Conclusions regarding democracy presented in this paper are in regards only to democracy as defined and compiled in Polity IV.

---

[26] This is a criterion that might arguably suggest a ranking of the US under its current administration below other western democracies.

[27] Although the further exploration of the democracy topic, like so many other topics briefly mentioned in this paper are very tempting.

The discussion now returns from this brief digression regarding definitions to the methodology of the democracy/economic output experiment. The democracy values used as input values for each country are modified several times in increments of 2 "democracy points". As briefly mentioned the democracy scale in Polity IVd ranges from 0 (no democracy) to 10 (full democracy). All other input variables are held constant, but 2, 4, and then 6 points are added and then subtracted from the democracy value in the input. Changes to the predicted economic output are recorded.

Results

The results of this exercise are presented numerically in the table, below.

Table 2: Predicted CGDP values at varying levels of democracy (2003).

Country	-6	-4	-2	Actual	+2	+4	+6
Canada	63.66	64.22	64.72	65.15	65.51	65.77	65.92
Cuba	10.75	11.10	11.46	11.88	12.37	12.94	13.60
Dominican Rep	14.44	14.81	15.23	15.71	16.28	16.93	17.67
Jamaica	27.22	27.81	28.49	29.25	30.05	30.88	31.69
Mexico	30.36	31.05	31.67	32.23	32.73	33.19	33.62
Nicaragua	4.97	5.21	5.60	6.16	6.87	7.74	8.72
Panama	46.23	46.53	46.86	47.23	47.61	47.98	48.34
Colombia	18.11	18.53	18.98	19.48	20.04	20.67	21.34
Venezuela	23.92	24.47	24.97	25.43	25.86	26.29	26.74
Ecuador	19.00	19.40	19.78	20.15	20.52	20.91	21.35
Peru	21.94	22.41	22.84	23.25	23.66	24.09	24.56
Brazil	24.08	24.53	24.92	25.26	25.57	25.89	26.22
Bolivia	10.00	10.70	11.41	12.09	12.75	13.38	13.98
Chile	30.01	30.50	30.93	31.32	31.69	32.06	32.45
Argentina	21.87	22.39	22.87	23.31	23.75	24.19	24.67
Belgium	62.09	62.94	63.77	64.56	65.27	65.88	66.38
Switzerland	28.12	28.67	29.33	30.08	30.89	31.73	32.59
Poland	44.65	45.04	45.45	45.86	46.26	46.63	46.96
Austria	61.43	61.99	62.47	62.87	63.18	63.39	63.49
Hungary	47.08	47.56	48.04	48.50	48.92	49.29	49.61
Italy	58.41	59.04	59.61	60.10	60.49	60.77	60.93
Albania	27.89	28.65	29.36	30.03	30.62	31.15	31.60

61

Macedonia	44.26	44.53	44.72	44.83	44.88	44.90	44.90
Slovenia	29.49	29.84	30.32	30.88	31.51	32.17	32.84
Greece	55.98	56.62	57.22	57.77	58.26	58.66	58.96
Cyprus	44.82	45.38	45.94	46.48	46.96	47.38	47.72
Russia	19.29	19.65	19.97	20.25	20.52	20.80	21.12
Estonia	32.00	32.32	32.72	33.19	33.71	34.27	34.85
Ukraine	16.36	16.56	16.82	17.18	17.62	18.14	18.72
Belarus	15.58	15.71	15.86	16.04	16.25	16.53	16.89
Armenia	3.73	4.27	4.83	5.40	5.97	6.51	7.03
Azerbaijan	17.62	17.79	17.99	18.23	18.55	18.96	19.45
Finland	64.09	64.69	65.21	65.63	65.94	66.13	66.21
Norway	66.72	67.20	67.60	67.91	68.12	68.23	68.25
Guinea-Bissau	2.46	2.41	2.32	2.21	2.12	2.07	2.09
Mali	8.54	9.03	9.56	10.13	10.75	11.44	12.23
Senegal	12.88	13.12	13.43	13.83	14.35	14.99	15.75
Benin	8.24	8.83	9.45	10.12	10.83	11.60	12.45
Liberia	0.06	0.06	0.06	0.06	0.06	0.06	0.06
Ghana	11.40	11.64	12.02	12.56	13.24	14.03	14.90
Gabon	24.58	25.14	25.68	26.20	26.68	27.12	27.53
Uganda	0.89	1.01	1.27	1.69	2.28	3.01	3.87
Kenya	12.99	13.35	13.75	14.22	14.77	15.40	16.10
Rwanda	-4.32	-4.02	-3.71	-3.41	-3.12	-2.83	-2.53
Somalia	6.26	6.26	6.26	6.26	6.26	6.26	6.26
Djibouti	-2.36	-2.38	-2.30	-2.11	-1.77	-1.26	-0.55
Eritrea	-8.58	-7.71	-6.80	-5.85	-4.87	-3.88	-2.88
Comoros	3.18	3.30	3.52	3.86	4.33	4.95	5.71
Tunisia	9.66	10.15	10.70	11.29	11.93	12.62	13.37
Iran	23.74	24.45	25.14	25.80	26.41	26.95	27.44
Turkey	32.76	33.29	33.79	34.27	34.73	35.20	35.68
Iraq	-7.65	-7.65	-7.65	-7.65	-7.65	-7.65	-7.65
Egypt	10.72	11.08	11.51	12.00	12.55	13.15	13.81
Syria	20.19	20.48	20.78	21.10	21.49	21.95	22.48
Jordan	2.42	2.78	3.29	3.92	4.66	5.47	6.33
Israel	53.13	53.84	54.48	55.03	55.48	55.81	56.02
Yemen	17.58	18.21	18.89	19.58	20.27	20.93	21.55
Afghanistan	11.91	11.91	11.91	11.91	11.91	11.91	11.91
Turkmenistan	15.08	15.51	15.95	16.39	16.87	17.39	17.96
Uzbekistan	4.23	4.54	4.87	5.24	5.68	6.20	6.80
China	34.39	34.73	35.09	35.48	35.89	36.32	36.78
Korea North	0.77	1.30	1.85	2.42	3.03	3.68	4.39
Japan	64.64	65.15	65.57	65.90	66.15	66.31	66.38
India	29.36	29.57	29.77	29.98	30.20	30.46	30.79
Pakistan	8.75	9.26	9.82	10.42	11.04	11.69	12.35
Laos	16.19	16.48	16.80	17.17	17.59	18.10	18.69
Papua New Guinea	32.30	32.95	33.65	34.39	35.14	35.88	36.61
Fiji	23.78	23.96	24.23	24.59	25.03	25.53	26.07
	1586.37	1614.13	1642.90	1672.68	1703.48	1735.32	1768.14

A further note on data ranges is in order at this point. Although the country's democracy value as defined in the Polity IVd data set is in a range from 0 to 10, the experimental democracy values used to produce the outputs in the table above can range from -6 to 16[28].

The results of this experiment as demonstrated by the numbers in the above table are very clear. In nearly all cases, democracy[29] is positively correlated with economic output. Only in the cases of Iraq and the Guinea-Bissau is there any question that democracy (and more democracy) is a "good" thing for the economies listed. To sum up the totals numerically, an increase in democracy of 6 points led to a steady predicted output growth of 5.7 %. A drop of 6 democracy points suggests an immediate drop of 5.4 % in economic output. Taken another way, around a one point change in democracy has a 1% impact on output.

Analysis

Although an about 5 % difference in economic output might not sound like a lot, in compounded terms it would make a tremendous difference on the well being a population. Consider, for example a comparison between one economy growing at 3 % per annum and another growing at 5% more, at 8%. After 20 years, the faster growing economy would be five times its original size while the slower growing one would have only doubled. If an economy were to go from low democracy (say a level of 1 or 2) to a high level of democracy, such a change might be an increase greater than 6 democracy "points" and therefore would further exceed the 5.x % expected increase in output. A change from 0 to 10 might result in around a 10% increase in output, according to the predictions of this model.

---

[28] In the case of countries with no democracies, subtracting 6 democracy "points" yields -6 and in cases where democracy is 10, a value of up to 16 can be achieved when using the methodology presented.
[29] As defined in Polity IV.

But what about Iraq and the Guinea-Bissau? Why were they not capable of growing in the prediction model? Iraq's continuous war and lack of regime make any growth at all a rather ridiculous concept. As soon as something is built up, it might be blown up again. As for the Guinea-Bissau, it experienced a coup during the year in question (2003) making any inferences regarding its non-conformance to the rest of the evidence difficult to determine[30].

It should be noted that the positive effect of democracy might still have a ceiling. The only claim, here, is that in the economies in the sample, the evidence appears to be that such a ceiling is not yet in sight.

Conclusion

This chapter presented the construction of a neural network model incorporating 28 economic and political factors to approximate economic output in any country. This model was then used to confirm conclusions that democracy has a positive and consistent impact on economic output. Even when applied outside the range of data used in their construction, neural networks can be utilized. Today's neural network models are capable of producing reasonable outputs even outside the range of expected values. Neural networks offer possibilities of analyzing complex processes such as economic growth. Standard analytical "models" such as the Solow growth model, or Cobb-Douglas production functions purposely make simplifying assumptions and focus on a very narrow set of input variables (typically 2). Neural network models can be used when complex interactions cannot be successfully simplified.

---

[30] Guinea-Bissau's democracy value for 2003 is listed as "1" and flagged for further review in the Polity IVd data set.

Chapter 5 Summary and Conclusions

The analyses of this paper have several interrelated dimensions. The computational viability of the recently re-accepted neural networks was reviewed and applied to empirical data. Simultaneously, a recent conclusion from the field of economic growth theory, that democracy has a weak but positive overall impact on growth was confirmed. The next few pages provide some final analysis of the data exercises in chapter 4, including potential avenues for further research using the current methodology and more broadly for the field of economic development. A short summary of the research is followed by conclusions and suggestions for further research. General observations are shared throughout.

Summary of Research

The (original?) research of this paper involved combining political and economic data series from 1950 to 2003 and removing time data to increase sample size. The Microsoft Neural Network was used on the data series to quantify the relationship of the democracy variable on economic output. The neural network created exhibited reasonable r^2 (0.73). The data analysis tools supplied by Microsoft SQL Server Analysis Services were successful in creating a neural network model summarizing the Polity IVd and Penn World Table data.

The democracy exercise and overviews of current neural network and economic growth fields in this paper provide a good starting point for further research. Solow type models, and many production functions, serve as a general reminder that economic growth is not a linear endeavor and might best be explored using more complex analytical techniques. Cobb-Douglas type production functions are not linear because of diminishing returns to scale. The model presented in chapter 4 computes a expected per capita GDP based on 28 political and economic variables.

Potential Further Research

The potential for further research with the current model and certainly with economic development generally are quite extensive. Immediate further research could be done with the current model.

The initial goal of using neural networks to understand economic development can be pursued further. One challenge in fine tuning the model is knowing when the model is performing well. Ironically, this is because getting the model to compute the exact economic output of a country is not the ideal case when not all potential inputs are included. If exact output were predicted while exogenous influences still impacted the country in question (say a famine, coup, volcanic eruption, etc...), then the model would by definition be computing output incorrectly since the exogenous influence would be unaccounted for.

There are certainly more factors that could be included to increase accuracy of the model. As mentioned, two oil rich nations (Saudi Arabia and Qatar) were excluded from the model. A separate neural network might be constructed to estimate output for those countries. Another curiosity of the model that might be explored is that if US output estimates are computed, they typically fall very short of the 100% value that would accurately describe its output. Instead estimates for the US by the models explored by the researcher tended to range from 55 % – 80% of its actual value. Estimates for higher output economies tended to be low.

Research actually using the model and focusing less on its mechanics, might be more practically beneficial. Countries with extremely unusual growth, or lack of growth, compared to their expected output should be researched to identify why they are not conforming to the expected outputs. Typically, when exploring differences in actual output vs. predicted it turns out that there was some type of revolution, or other inherent problem (like geography) with the country appears to prohibit its growth.

With respect to the democracy question in the study conducted in chapter 4, research could be continued by including the "autocracy" variable which is complementary to democracy. Since the power void of a democracy loss, for example, may eventually be filled with a more totalitarian power base an increase in autocracy may reduce the impact of democracy. The model exhibited in chapter 4 does not consider autocracy[31].

The models could be re-constructed using only later data instead of all the way back to 1950. If "technology" really has as large an effect as some growth research claims, that would argue for the emphasis on more current data. Unfortunately, this would lead to the loss of many valuable input cases which was part of the point of the methodology used in this study. Historical data should have a dampening effect on CGDP model output variables in later years if technology or productivity is increasing in most of the countries in the data. It is suspected, however, that many countries especially in the existing data set have not reached the point at which they are rapidly

---

[31] In fact, accuracy of the model predictions decreased when autocracy was included in several tests.

increasing their productivity considering that their output is often stagnant. Some research has been done

More political institution data such as data on property right protection could be added to the model. As was mentioned in chapter 4, the definition of the democracy value in Polity IV already contains some political institution information. This fact actually makes the model even more cutting edge since the more recent political economy research in regards to growth began emphasizing institutions a few years ago.

Another modification that could be made to the model would be to multiply CGDP by population. This would result in a production function for GDP which might be useful in some circumstances.

One strength of the commercial software package used in this data analysis is that it allows researchers to add their own algorithms (written in C++, C#, VB, and other languages) to the analysis framework. Other algorithms can then be compared side by side as with the three models in this study. In relation to the software, several data visualization components were recently released for Microsoft SQL Server Analysis Services. These components might make it easier to understand some of the neural network behavior and the data generally.

Clusters of similar countries could be targeted for research. A look at clusters of countries could result in different formulas and different variables that are more influential in certain countries. For example, in a countries initial growth period, increases in basic infrastructure or other variables might have a greater impact than in more developed countries. Grouping countries into groups that appear to behave similarly might make it possible to recommend better growth strategies for other countries that have the same political and economic profiles. More alarmingly, it is unrealistic to think that any one variable potentially involved in economic development will have a positive or negative impact on all countries in all scenarios. Analyzing countries in clusters as enough data on countries in those clusters is available will lead to better understanding.

The potential for progress with the framework used in this paper combined with the underprivileged existence of billions of the world's people makes it difficult to stop both the research and the even the thoughts of how such research might be enhanced.

General Further Research and Concluding Remarks

Economic growth and political science researchers have managed to amass sizable quantities of data which contain at least historic data that may be able to assist policy makers and analysts in making recommendations and making decisions. Through the utilization of automated data analysis techniques, policy makers and citizens could potentially be presented with more optimal strategies to enhance the likelihood of economic success and the reduction of poverty.

New researchers looking at economic growth are welcomed to the field by the overwhelming quantity of data.[32] When they seek out some theory to enlighten them, or take a class, they are shown the Solow model from the 1950s and left potentially more confused than before. Standardized data sets like Polity which is supported by government grants and the Penn World Tables are a refreshing foundation in the otherwise seemingly unorganized endeavor of understanding economic development. Perhaps more directed research teams targeting specific variables and with a lesser emphasis on "growth" over "development" could clear up some of the scholarly disagreements that still appear to exist between growth studies. It is hoped that this

---

[32] Both by the number of potential variables, and then by problems with candidate data.

work will contribute to the further acceptance of neural networks and future computational techniques in the fields of political science and economics.

References

Acemoglu, Daron, Simon Johnson and James Robinson. "Institutions as the Fundamental Cause of Long-Run Growth." Massachusetts Institute of Technology. April 29, 2004. <http://econ-www.mit.edu/faculty/download_pdf.php?id=1183> (cited April 20, 2007)[33].

Aiken, Milam. "Using a Neural Network to Forecast Inflation." *Industrial Management & Data Systems* 99, no. 7 (1999): 296-301.

Alesina, Alberto and Roberto Perotti. "Income Distribution, Political Instability, and Investment." National Bureau of Economic Research. Working Paper no. W4486 (October 1993).

Alesina, Alberto, Sule Özler, Nouriel Roubini and Phillip Swage. "Political Instability and economic growth." *Journal of Economic Growth* 1, no. 2 (June 1996): 189-211.

Barbieri, Katherine. "Economic Interdependence: A Path to Peace or a Source of International Conflict." *Journal of Peace Research* 33, no. 1 (February 1996): 29-49.

Barro, Robert and Rachel McCleary. "Religion and Economic Growth." National Bureau of Economic Research. Working Paper no. 9682 (April 2003).

Bénassy-Quéré, Agnès, Maylis Coupet and Thierry Mayer. "Institutional Determinants of Foreign Direct Investment." CEPII Working Paper No 2005-05. April 2005. <http://www.cerdi.org/Colloque/AFSE2005/papier/Benassy_Mayer.pdf > (Cited April 20, 2007).

Cybenko, G. "Approximation by Superpositions of a Sigmoidal Function." *Mathematics of Control, Signals, and Systems* 2 (1989): 303-314.

Collier, Paul and Jan Willem Gunning. "Explaining African Economic Performance." *Journal of Economic Literature* 37, no. 1 (March 1999): 64-111.

DeLong, Bradley. Review of William Easterly's *The Elusive Quest for Growth* <http://econ161.berkeley.edu/TotW/Easterly_neoliberal.html> (cited Dec. 7,

---

[33] This work was published in several formats; the cited version was prepared for the *Handbook of Economic Growth* edited by Philippe Aghion and Steven Durlauf which was published by North-Holland/Elsevier in 2005.

2003).

Doepke, Mathias. "Lecture notes on the neoclassical growth model." <http://www.econ.ucla.edu/doepke/teaching/c32/sec2.pdf> (cited April 14, 2007).

Durlauf, Steven, Paul Johnson and Jonathan Temple. "Growth Econometrics." Vassar College Economics Working Paper # 61. October 22, 2004. <http://irving.vassar.edu/vcewp/vcewp61.pdf> (cited April 20, 2007).

Easterly, William. *The Elusive Quest for Growth: Economists' Adventures and Misadventures in the Tropics.* Cambridge, MA: MIT Press, 2001.

Easterly, William and Ross Levine. "Africa's Growth Tragedy: Policies and Ethnic Divisions." *The Quarterly Journal of Economics* 112, no. 4 (November 1997): 1203-1250.

Esquivel, Gerardo and Felipe Larrain. "The Impact of G-3 Exchange Rate Volatility on Developing Countries." G-24 Discussion Paper 16. Geneva: United Nations Conference on Trade and Development, January 2002.

Evans, Peter and James Rauch. "Bureaucracy and Growth: A Cross-National Analysis of the Effects of 'Weberian' State Structures on Economic Growth." *American Sociological Review* 64, no. 5 (October 1999): 748-765.

Feng, Yi. *Democracy, Governance, and Economic Performance.* Cambridge, MA: MIT Press, 2003.

Fraser, Christopher. "Neural Networks: Literature Review from a Statistical Perspective." California State University, Hayward. Spring 2000. <http://www.sci.csuhayward.edu/statistics/Neural/cfprojnn.htm> (cited August 12, 2006).

Fine, Terrence L. *Feedforward Neural Network Methodology.* New York, NY: Springer, 1999.

Fosu, Augustin Kwasi. "Political Instability and Export Performance in Sub-Saharan Africa." *Review of Economics and Statistics* 79, no. 4 (November 1997): 540-550.

Funahashi, Ken-Ichi. "On the Approximate Realization of Continuous Mappings by Neural Networks." *Neural Networks* 2 (1989): 183-192.

Hayami, Yujiro and Yoshihisa Godo. *Development Economics.* New York: Oxford University Press, 2005.

Helpman, Elhanan. *The Mystery of Economic Growth.* Cambridge, MA: Harvard University Press, 2004.

Hopfield, John. "Neural Networks and Physical Systems with Emergent Collective Computational Abilities." *Proceedings of the National Academy of Sciences of the USA*, 79 (1982): 2554-2558.

Hornik, Kurt, Maxwell Stinchcombe, and Halbert White. "Multi-layer Feedforward Networks are Universal Approximators." *Neural Networks* 2 (1989): 359-366.

Jones, Charles. *Introduction to Economic Growth*. New York: WW North, 1998.

King, Gary. "Improving Forecasts of State Failure." *World Politics* 53, no. 4 (July 2001): 623-658.

Lucas, Robert Jr. "On the Mechanics of Economic Development." *Journal of Monetary Economics* 22, no. 1 (July 1988): 3-42.

MacLennan, Jamie and ZhaoHui Tan. *Data Mining with SQL Server 2005*. Indianapolis, IN: Wiley, 2005.

Marshall, Monty and Keith Jaggers. *Polity IV Project: Dataset Users' Manual*. University of Maryland, College Park. 2002. Available from <http://www.cidcm.umd.edu/inscr/polity> (cited August 5, 2007).

Mankiw, N. Gregory, David Romer, and David Weil. "A Contribution to the Empirics of Economic Growth." *The Quarterly Journal of Economics* 107, no. 2 (May 1992): 407-437.

Maren, Alianna, Craig Harston, and Robert Pap (ed). *Handbook of Neural Computing Applications*. San Diego, CA: Academic Press, 1990.

McCulloch, Warren and Walter Pitts. "A Logical Calculus of the Ideas Immanent in Nervous Activity." *Bulletin of Mathematical Biology* 5, no. 4 (December 1943): 115-133.

Miguel, Edward, Shanker Satyanath, and Ernest Sergenti. "Economic Shocks and Civil Conflict: An Instrumental Variables Approach." *Journal of Political Economy* 112, no. 4 (2004): 725–753.

Mousseau, Michael. "Market Prosperity, Democratic Consolidation, and Democratic Peace." *The Journal of Conflict Resolution* 44, no. 4 (August 2000): 472-507.

North, Douglas. "Institutions." *Journal of Economic Perspectives* 5, no. 1 (Winter 1991): 97-112.

Olazaran, Mikel. "A Sociological Study of the Official History of the Perceptrons Controversy." *Social Studies of Science* 26, no. 3 (August 1996): 611-659.

Pack, Howard. "Endogenous Growth Theory: Intellectual Appeal and Empirical Shortcomings." *The Journal of Economic Perspectives* 8, no. 1 (Winter, 1994): 55-72.

Quinn, Dennis and John Woolley. "Democracy and National Economic Performance: The Preference for Stability." *American Journal of Political Science* 45, no. 3 (July 2001): 634-657.

Rodrik, Dani. "Getting Institutions Right." Harvard University. April 2004. < http://ksghome.harvard.edu/~drodrik/ifo-institutions%20article%20_April%202004_.pdf > (cited April 20, 2007).

Rodrik, Dani, Arvind Subramanian and Francesco Trebbi. "Institutions Rule: The Primacy of Institutions Over Geography and Integration in Economic Development." *Journal of Economic Growth* 9, no. 2 (June 2004).

Romer, Paul. "Endogenous Technological Change." *Journal of Political Economy* 98, no. 5, Part 2: The Problem of Development: A Conference on the Institute for the Study of Free Enterprise Systems (October 1990): S71 – S102.

Solow, Robert. "A Contribution to the Theory of Economic Growth." *The Quarterly Journal of Economics* 70, no. 1 (January 1956): 65-94.

Solow, Robert. "Technical Change and the Aggregate Production Function." *The Review of Economics and Statistics* 39, no. 3 (August 1957): 312-320.

Swanson, Norman and Halbert White. "A Model Selection Approach to Real-Time Macroeconomic Forecasting Using Linear Models and Artificial Neural Networks." *Review of Economics and Statistics* 79, no. 4 (November 1997): 540-550.

Taylor, John. "Teaching Modern Macroeconomics at the Principles Level." *The American Economic Review* 90, no. 2 (May 2000): 90-94.

Taylor, J.G. (ed.) *Mathematical Approaches to Neural Networks*. Amsterdam: Elsevier Science Publishers, 1993.

Tkacz, Greg. "Neural Network Forecasting of Canadian GDP Growth." *International Journal of Forecasting* 17, no. 1 (January-March 2001): 57-69.

Varshney, Ashutosh. "Democracy vs. Growth in India." *Foreign Affairs* 86, no. 2 (March-April 2007): 93-106.

Vogt, Andrew and Joe Bared. "Accident Models for Two-Lane Rural Roads: Segments and Intersections." Publication No. FHWA-RD-98-133. US Department of

Transportation, 1998.

Warner, Brad and Manavendra Misra. "Understanding Neural Networks as Statistical Tools." *The American Statistician* 40, no. 4 (November 1996): 284-293.